The First
New York-Philadelphia
Stage Road

This perfectly preserved Conestoga wagon displayed at the Farmers Museum in the Landis Valley, north of Lancaster, Pa., carried powder and ammunition to Commodore Perry at the battle of Lake Erie in 1812.

The First New York- Philadelphia Stage Road

James and Margaret Cawley

Photographs by the authors

Rutherford • Madison • Teaneck
Fairleigh Dickinson University Press
London and Toronto: Associated University Presses

Also by James and Margaret Cawley

Historic New Jersey In Pictures
Exploring the Little Rivers of New Jersey
Along the Old York Road
Along the Delaware and Raritan Canal
Tales of Old Grafton
Exploring the Housatonic River and Valley

Associated University Presses, Inc.
4 Cornwall Drive
East Brunswick, New Jersey 08816

Associated University Presses Ltd.
69 Fleet Street
London EC4Y 1EU, England

Associated University Presses
Toronto M5E 1A7, Canada

Library of Congress Cataloging in Publication Data
Cawley, James S
The first New York-Philadelphia stage road.

Bibliography: p.
1. King's Highway, N.J. and Pa.–History. 2. New
Jersey–History, Local. 3. Pennsylvania–History, Local.
4. Historic sites–New Jersey. 5. Historic
sites–Pennsylvania. I. Cawley, Margaret, joint author.
II. Title.
HE356.K56C38   388.1'09749   78–75175
ISBN   0–8386–2331–X

Printed in the United States of America

8 11 886 ✓

Contents

Introduction

The early colonial roads were built on cleared and widened Indian paths, which had previously been the only avenues of overland travel.

One such road, the first to be built to the north out of Philadelphia, was built on one such path. It was known as the Falls Indian path between Philadelphia and Morrisville, Pennsylvania. That road later became a part of the King's Highway between Philadelphia and Elizabethtowne Point on Newark Bay.

Today the route of the original road is a confusion of city streets and country roads, and much of it has disappeared entirely.

The charm, slower pace, and way of life that marked the days of the stagecoach are gone, of course. However, the many landmarks, some of which are over three hundred years old, may be found on or near the old road.

The King's Highway played an important part in the development of New Jersey, eastern Pennsylvania, and the cities of Philadelphia and New York.

The First
New York-Philadelphia
Stage Road

A land without a history is like a man without a memory.
        Woodrow Wilson

1

The Need for and the Building of the Road

THE glowing accounts about the opportunities for trade and settlement in America told by Henry Hudson to his employers, the United East India Company of Holland, resulted in a wave of emigration to this country during the early years of the seventeenth century. The arrivals settled on Long Island and Manhattan and along the shore of the Hudson River in what is now Bergen County, New Jersey. Later groups settled along the shores of the Delaware and Schuylkill rivers in the area of present-day Philadelphia.

During the early days of those river and coastal settlements, communication between settlements was limited to sailing vessels and small craft over inland waters.

In the building of the early roads it was the custom to clear and widen the Indian paths as a base. One such road, the subject of our story, was the first road built to the north out of Philadelphia. It extended between Philadelphia and Morrisville, Pennsylvania, along the west shore of the Delaware River. That section became a part of the King's Highway between Philadelphia and Elizabeth-towne Point. The road later became known as the Upper Road to distinguish it from the Lawrie Road between Burlington and Perth Amboy.

Stage and other travellers bound for Manhattan embarked

on a sailing ferry at the end of the road at Elizabeth-towne Point.

The settlers lived on what they raised, and there was little need for outside markets for their farm products during the early years. At most gristmills there was usually a store where farm products could be traded for essentials such as salt and molasses, which were not raised on the farms. Sometimes a blacksmith shop was operated near the mill where nails, hinges, and other iron items could be fashioned.

As more arrivals came to America, living conditions, particularly in the matter of housing, became acute in some of the coastal settlements. Many of the late-comers in the lower river settlements were forced to live in caves or crude brush shelters the first winter of their stay.

It was the desire of the majority of settlers to move into the wilderness, where plenty of land could be had for the taking. However, there was a general belief and fear that to do so would be risking attack from hostile Indians and wild animals. Such fears were intensified by the reports brought into the settlements by pack-train drivers and hunters, such as the following entry in one of the diaries of early Elizabeth-towne settlers in Theodore Thayer's book *As We Were:* "During the cold winter nights the howls of wolves and the screams of panthers and the savages could be heard." Such tales quickly spread throughout the overcrowded coastal settlements.

Despite their fears of the wild interior, many of the coastal and river settlers were forced to move inland to take up land on which they could raise crops to feed their families. They found the travelling overland through the dense wilderness difficult. Many of them had to carry essential tools such as a broad axe and their seeds as well as their few household possessions on the backs of the family. Others who owned an oxen or pack horse found the going much easier and faster.

After much of the interior land had been taken up, a need for gristmills developed. One of the earliest of the mills was Worth's, located on the shore of Stony Brook in Lawrence Township in New Jersey. That mill served the farmers for a radius of forty miles, grinding their grain into flour. In order to get their grain to the mills in the two-wheel ox-drawn carts, "ways" were built from the farms to the nearest mill. Worth's was typical of the many mills with their surrounding small settlements along the King's Highway. From such small beginings grew many larger communities such as Princeton, Trenton, Philadelphia, and others.

With more land cleared and more acreage planted, a need for outside markets developed to which the surplus crops, beyond the family needs, could be sold. To reach such markets, roads to replace the crude "ways" became a pressing need in most sections of New Jersey and eastern Pennsylvania.

The authorization for the first approved section of the stage road was by the New Jersey Proprietors in 1665 between Elizabethtowne Point to the Raritan River at what is now Highland Park, New Jersey. At about the same time the Pennsylvania Assembly authorized the building of the road extending north from Philadelphia to Morrisville, Pennsylvania. This section of road was later to become a part of the stage road between Elizabethtowne and Philadelphia.

The specifications called for a road four chains or ninety-nine feet in width. However, since there was no need at the time for roads of that width, few if any of the early colonial roads adhered to those specifications.

Soon after the appointment of the road boards, it was decided that the most-needed road was one connecting Elizabeth-towne with Rahway, Woodbury, Piscataway, and the ferry across the Raritan River at Highland Park.

The colonial custom of naming officially approved roads the King's Highway has resulted in some confusion among students of history as there are several so named in New Jersey and Pennsylvania. For example, the King's Highway that is most frequently confused with the subject of our story is the one that passes through Camden, New Jersey, across the river from Philadelphia.

It was agreed that the easiest way to build the section of

13

the road to the Raritan River was to clear and widen the Assunpink Indian path and build the road over it.

It was a sound decision to build over the ancient Indian paths. As was true of all Indian paths, they had been laid out taking advantage of the easiest grades, ascending the hills by the best routes, avoiding the marshy places, and crossing the streams at fording places least likely to become flooded when the streams were high.

Black powder for blasting, picks and shovels, horse or oxen-drawn scrapers were the only road-building tools available.

Later John Inian, together with some associates, bought a thousand acres of land, bordering the road route between the Raritan River and Kingston and began building an extension to the road to the Millstone River at Kingston. They hoped to sell land to the new settlers coming into the valley from the upper Hudson valley.

The plans for the road included the eventual completion of the road to Trenton. Pennsylvania earlier approved the building of the rest of the road, along the west shore of the Delaware River from Philadelphia to Morrisville.

Until the road was completed, shortly after the end of the seventeenth century, vehicular travel was uncomfortable in any type of vehicle. That situation was considerably changed when the legislatures of both Pennsylvania and New Jersey appointed committees to "inspect the new road and remove all bowlders and tree stumps and to bridge all streams between Philadelphia and Elizabeth-towne Point."

During the early years of the first quarter of the eighteenth century, when the above improvements had been completed, it was possible for four-wheeled vehicles, including the stage wagons, to travel over the road in comparative comfort, except during the mud season, of course. The King's Highway thus became the first vehicular road between Philadelphia and Elizabeth-towne Point. A short ride on the sailing ferry from the latter place carried travellers to the Battery in Manhattan.

It would seem in order at this point in our story to outline in detail, for those readers who may want to orient themselves while reading this book or perhaps those who may want to follow it by car, that part of the road that may be followed today. Much of the old road between Rahway, Woodbridge, Piscataway, and the Raritan River has been eliminated by such highways as the Garden State, New Jersey Turnpike, and others. Because of new municipal streets in Woodbridge, Piscataway, and Rahway, one cannot locate the road as it was. Even the town engineers cannot help.

However, one may drive today from Elizabethport (formerly Elizabeth-towne Point), where the remains of the old ferry landing may be seen.

Drive west on East Jersey Street to Elizabeth. Follow Route 27 from Elizabeth through Rahway to the Raritan River at Highland Park. That part of Route 27 from Elizabeth to Rahway is over the route of the old road, but from Rahway to the river it is not.

From New Brunswick, across the Raritan River, follow Route 27 again to Kingston and the Millstone River. Cross the river to the Kingston-Princeton road and follow that to and through Princeton, past Morven, the former home of Richard Stockton, and from there follow Route 206 to and through Lawrenceville to the Battle Monument in Trenton.

The route herein described follows closely the route of the old road with the exceptions noted in the following text.

From the Battle Monument, drive south on Warren Street to the corner of Ferry Street. The Eagle Tavern, built in 1765, still stands at that point. The tavern is in poor repair, but there are some plans being considered for its complete restoration as it was during the days of the stages.

From the river bridge, follow the river road in Pennsylvania south past the old ferry house and the site of the early trading post.

A mile or so south of Morrisville, the sand and gravel operations have wiped out entirely the old road to Tullytown.

Turn right above the gravel works and over to the Delaware

15

Expressway. Follow that south and turn left into Tullytown. Follow old Route 13 to and through Bristol where a right turn is made to get to the Delaware Expressway again. Follow the Expressway through Frankford and to Market Street in Philadelphia.

Don't fail to plan a day of exploration of the restored mile-square former industrial slum area, known as Society Hill. It can be entered at any point between the Delaware River and Ninth Street.

There are plenty of interesting places and things to see in Society Hill. Among them is the well known Head House on Pine Street, built in 1745, the end of which was formerly a fire house. Another is the restored A Man Full Of Trouble Tavern that may be seen below the multi-story Alcoa Towers on Second Street. A hundred or more of the eighteenth-century, three-story brick homes have been restored and are fully occupied. The narrow-cobbled Delancy Street is today as it has been during the past century or longer.

Across the street from the Head House is an eighteenth-century pharmacy which is interesting to visit. Altogether, Society Hill is fascinating with endless opportunities for the photographer.

2

Stage Wagons and Other Type Vehicles

IT was not until near the end of the first quarter of the eighteenth century that vehicles could traverse the entire road.

Before improvements were completed on the lower part of the road, in Pennsylvania William Penn preferred to travel between his country estate at Pennsbury Manor and Philadelphia in his sailing barge, rather than over the road in his two-wheel chaise.

A somewhat similar situation existed from the fact that, before improvements were completed on the Trenton-Elizabeth-towne section, many travelers found it easier and more comfortable to make part of the journey between Manhattan and Perth Amboy by sailing vessel through the long reaches of the Arthur Kill. Depending upon the tide and wind, the sailing journey added as much as two days to the journey. It is said that Benjamin Franklin, on one of his journeys between Boston and Philadelphia, did in fact use the sailing-vessel ferry and lost over two days.

Even as late as the middle of the eighteenth century, when stage companies were providing regular service, one traveller described a stage journey as "the discomfort that had to be endured over a break neck road, crushed, shaken, thrown about and bumped," an adventure he did not care to repeat.

During those early years in the winter months many travelers in stage coaches and private vehicles preferred to use the road because the regularly rolled and hard-packed snow made the ride exceptionally smooth. Sled runners were substituted for the wheels, and during such smoother journeys passengers found the traveling much pleasanter than during the other seasons. They were not crushed, shaken, thrown about, and bumped.

The early stage wagons were straight-sided farm wagons across the sides of which were fashioned three or four wooden seats without backs. To reach the rear seat, passengers had to climb over the forward seats and the passengers in them. There were no springs or slings to reduce jolting and sway, and the wheels were fastened to the wooden axles with linchpins. A bucket of tar was slung under the wagon to use as lubricant on the axles. Frequently a linchpin would fall out, spilling the passengers and their baggage in a heap on the floor of the stage. Fastened to the sides of the wagon were a half dozen hickory hoops over which were stretched covers of homespun cloth.

It must have been difficult for one who had to travel and endure the discomforts of the journey to believe it was possible to devise a more uncomfortable way to travel overland. The alternative was to travel by sailing vessel; that sometimes required a week longer, depending upon wind and tide. On stage journeys during the rainy season, passengers had to frequently get out and manhandle the horses and stage out of deep mud holes and marshlands.

One of the first stage lines to offer regular service between Trenton and New Brunswick advertised in the *American Weekly Mercury* in the January 31, 1738, issue as follows:

TO ACCOMODATE THE PUBLIC there will be a stage wagon that will set out from Trenton to New Brunswick over the King's Highway twice a week and back again during the summer. It will be fitted with benches covered over, so that passengers may sit easy and dry, and care will be taken to deliver goods and messages safe. . . . every passenger to pay two shillings and six pence. Goods and parcels carried at the lowest rates.

The highlight of stage travel was the establishment of the John Mercereau Stage Line, which reduced the running time between the two terminals by a day and a half. The Mercereau line was called "the Line of the Flying Machine," but his stages were still the farm wagons with board seats. However, the fancy name and the promise of saving so much time on the run attracted enough customers to necessitate adding more stages to accommodate them.

The penalty for the faster time was riding until late at night instead of the usual custom of sundown stops and starts at sunrise. That meant late suppers and fast breakfasts.

It was not until after the Revolutionary War that the larger and far more comfortable Concord coaches began operating on the road. Instead of drafty and inadequate side curtains used on the earlier farm wagons, the Concords were fully enclosed to protect the passengers from bad weather. Because the Concords were slung on heavy leather slings, they had less side sway. The comfort of the Concord coaches, compared to the earlier stages, was as much of an improvement as that of modern cars over the model-T Fords.

One of the first lines to use the new Concords was the Joseph Hart Stage Line, which advertised them in 1772 as follows:

The Philadelphia stage coach, a very pleasant, easy and delightful carriage will set out for New York by way of Bristol, Trenton and Elizabeth-towne Point. The price will be thirty shillings for each passenger.

Thus it had required nearly three quarters of a century before stage travel provided any degree of comfort for the passenger.

By the third quarter of the eighteenth century, stage and private vehicular travel had increased considerably.

A new type of vehicle began using the road, adding still more to the already heavy traffic. It was the famous Conestoga wagon made by a Mr. Gingrich, whose shop was located in Lancaster County, Pennsylvania. The name Conestoga has been given to an Indian group, to the valley where the wagons were made, and to a creek and many other places and things.

As the demand for Conestoga wagons increased, Mr. Gingrich soon had to enlarge his small shop to a much larger factory. There were craftsmen, wheelwrights, joiners, and turners available in Lancaster County. Aside from the use of a saw and a turning lathe, everything about the Conestoga wagon was homemade with hand tools. The wagon bed measured sixteen feet in length and four feet in width. The ends were higher than the center, and the body was shaped like a boat and was waterproof. On the wheels were iron rims a half inch thick and four to ten inches wide.

With its final coat of Prussian blue paint on the body, bright red running gear, and a white homespun cloth top, it weighed three thousand pounds and cost two hundred and fifty dollars. The wagons could carry thirty barrels of flour and five hogshead of other perishables.

When on the road the horses carried, in a metal frame attached to the head harness, a set of musical bells.

The fleets of the Conestoga wagons going down the King's Highway must have been a thrilling sight.

The finest example of a Conestoga wagon we know of may be seen at the Farmer's Museum near Lancaster, Pennsylvania. According to tradition, it was that very wagon that carried powder from the Du Pont mills on Brandywine Creek to Commodore Perry during the battle of Lake Erie in 1812. The wagon is in perfect condition as may be seen in the illustration. It seems possible, despite its age, that the wagon could make the journey again.

The Conestoga wagons were the freight carriers throughout the colonies during the period from 1772 to 1849. From then

20

on, of course, they carried the families and the gold hunters across the continent to the West Coast.

Following the signing of the peace treaty with England in 1783, a gradual restoration of nonmilitary traffic began to crowd the road, and the traffic was soon far greater than before the war. The rapid growth of New York and Philadelphia was largely responsible.

More of the elegant Concord stages could be seen on the road. They were embellished with vivid colors, and some were lavishly striped with gold leaf. The harness on the four horses was very fancy, and the brass fittings gleamed.

Fixed to each side of the coach was a board bearing the name of a ship. The inside of the coach was called the cabin and the driver's seat the deck.

Not long after the Concords began to use the new road, the crude farm-wagon stages disappeared.

One of the most spectacular sights during the early coaching days on the King's Highway must have been the gathering of 168 relief stage horses at Kingston in 1824–25, when the Marquis de Lafayette toured America. The General passed through Kingston on his way to review the troops, assembled at Trenton to do him honor. He rode in a splendid barouche, drawn by six gray horses.

To conclude this chapter with no reference to the "kings" of the road, usually addressed as captain, would, in our opinion, leave the story incomplete. The reference to the "kings" is not intended to include the drivers of the earlier farm-wagon stages but rather to the drivers of the beautiful Concord coaches.

The title of captain was believed derived from the naval nomenclature used for the coach.

The drivers of the Concord coaches wore, as a rule and depending upon the weather, a large high-crowned beaver hat, a calfskin coat that reached to the top of their highly polished boots and, to top it all, a long bright red scarf around his waist.

Carrying the mail from village to village, or when stopping

21

for a change of horses, the drivers were usually surrounded by people eager for the latest news about events in other villages along the stage route.

One early writer described the arrival of the stages at his small New Jersey village in this way: "When the stage approached our village, behind the magnificent horses, spurred on by blast on a bugle, the crash of the wheels of the towering equipage raised a huge cloud of dust. It all made an inspiring sight that electrified everyone who witnessed it."

3

The Stage Taverns

Long ago at the end of the route,
The stage pulled up and the folks stepped out.
They have all passed under the tavern door,
The youth and his bride and the three scores.
Their eyes were weary with dust and gleam,
The day has gone like an empty dream,
Soft may they slumber, and trouble no more,
For their eager journey, its jolt and roar,
In the old stage coach over the mountain.
                                    Author unknown

DURING colonial times the taverns, ordinaries, and inns, as they were variously known, depending upon their location, were very important places to the stage passengers. The discomfort of the journey was quickly forgotten, particularly at the better-class taverns where good accomodations, food, and drink were served. During cold weather a good fire in the keeping (sitting) room also helped to restore the cheerfulness of the passengers.

The taverns played an equally important part in the lives of the people of the communities along the stage route in that they afforded some relief from the day-long services in the meeting houses, particularly during the winter weather.

In view of that it is easy to understand why, wherever there was a meeting house a tavern was not too far away. It was common practice for the men, during the noon day break in the services, to repair to the tavern for a warming drink or two. The women had to be content to stay in the meeting house, getting what comfort they could from their foot warmers that had been filled with hot coals from their home fireplaces. The men brought a new supply of hot coals from the tavern when they returned to the meeting house for the afternoon service.

The taverns built before the Revolutionary War were of two classes: one to accomodate stage passengers and the other for the accomodation of wagoners and drovers. The latter usually provided large areas of feeding grounds for the cattle.

The tavern, wherever it was located, was the center of most social gatherings as there were no other buildings in most communities large enough to accomodate large groups of people. Town meetings were sometimes held in the local tavern each spring.

Before the beginning of the Revolutionary War the taverns were also the meeting places of the Committee of Safety. The dispatch riders also left their messages to be picked up by other riders to carry to other communities. The landlords as a rule were sympathetic to the cause of the patriots throughout the colonies. In many communities, church meetings were held in nearby taverns. That practice was followed by the First Presbyterian Church of Lawrenceville, New Jersey. Their parish meetings were held across the King's Highway in the Cock and Bull Tavern. That tavern is still standing and is now a private residence.

Throughout the provinces of the Jerseys, bordering on the old road, accomodations were provided for overnight guests as soon as the road became passable. At first, travellers were lodged and fed in private homes along the way.

To encourage people of good character to open public houses, legislation was enacted in 1768 ordering all communities on the stage road to provide a tavern for the relief and entertainment of strangers.

However, until there was sufficient income from the operation of the taverns, many tavern owners had to supplement their income with other employment.

As the increased travel called for more and better overnight accomodations and meals, more stringent legislation was enacted governing license requirements and how the tavern had to be conducted. The new laws prohibited gambling, tippling, drunkenness, and other vices "to the scandal of religion."

Constables regularly inspected all taverns there after and, following the new regulations, fixed rates for rooms, board, and refreshment, the prices for which had to be posted in every tavern. A further requirement was the posting of a bond of twenty pounds and the endorsement, in the form of letters from six local citizens, testifying to the character of the applicant.

In 1787 there were over one hundred taverns on the King's Highway between Elizabeth-towne and Philadelphia.

In sharp contrast to the often wretched accomodations offered in the earlier years, the newer taverns provided better accomodations, meals, and refreshment as the end of the century neared.

The better-class taverns vied with the less pretentious through elegant furnishings, and in some of the newer taverns fireplaces were provided in every guest room in contrast to most of the earlier taverns, where the only heated room was the keeping or sitting room downstairs, which travellers were reluctant, in the winter, to leave and go to their rooms. The usual small bar in the keeping room was also a delaying factor.

In the corner of the keeping room in a New Jersey tavern was posted this sign:

All ye who stand before this fire pray sit ye down; tis my desire that other folks as well as you should see the fire and feel it too.

Evening gatherings in many of the taverns were apparently a lot of fun as the following indicates:

As the hours passed the noise became louder and more contagious. The landlord's good whiskey undoubtedly contributed quite a bit to the hilarity. Long before midnight the uproar usually became terrific. The dim light from a few candles in sconces on the walls was almost obscured by the dust that rose from the floor and from smoke from innumerable pipes. The landlord stood behind the corner bar with a pleased look, for he knew the louder the merriment, the greater would be his profit.

A spirited contest was going on between two dancers until one of them was compelled to stop from sheer exhaustion.

Such affairs usually ended with the winners of the various contests inviting all those assembled to join them for a drink at the bar.

Then there was the story describing a typical evening by the teamsters of the Conestoga wagons and perhaps joined by some of the cattle drovers staying at the tavern as it was described by Mr. John Onswake in his delightful book, *The Conestoga Six-horse Bell Teams of Eastern Pennsylvania.*

The wagoners were a noisy, jolly crew who loved to frolic and dance at the end of the day while their horses stood contentedly eating the grass in the corrals.

The music of the violins was usually heard inside the tavern and many of the drivers, who had walked the greater part of the twenty or more miles they had travelled that day, danced all evening. Such tunes as the *Virginia Reel,* the *French Reel, Four Square, Jim Crow,* and others were played. Monongahela whiskey was served at three cents a glass.

In compliance with the Duke of York's laws in the Jersey provinces, tavern owners were required to display signs in front of all taverns. Many of the signs were truly works of art. Some of them featured portraits of famous people such as George Washington (Washington Inn), or an animal (the Black Cat Tavern), or perhaps a symbol in the form of crossed keys (the Crossed Keys Tavern).

An English visitor to Philadelphia, during the mid-seventeenth century, remarked about the signs on the taverns and stores throughout the city. Such signs as Noah's Art, Bunyon's Pilgrim, A Man Full Of Trouble, and many others. The visitor felt very much at home as the custom of such signs on taverns and stores originated in England.

Within a few years after the middle of the seventeenth century, there were so many signs displayed that they were declared a public nuisance by the city fathers and ordered removed. That is, all signs except those on taverns.

The old signs, many of which had been painted by well-known artists, have become so valuable that they are treasured collection in such places as the Mercer Museum in Doylestown, Pennsylvania, where possibly the largest collection in America may be seen. Many others are in private collections.

Another type of tavern sign graced the entrance to many roadside public houses along the King's Highway. Those signs exhibited quite a range of country humor for the stage passengers. Following are a few examples.

I William McDermott live here, I sell good liquor, ale or beer, I've made my sign a little wider To let you know I sell good cider.

Another sign read:

The rule of this house and it can't be broken, Is to pay on delivery and not give trust, I've trusted many to my sorrow, Pay today, I'll trust tomorrow,

One of our favorite signs was displayed in front of the Beehive Tavern in Kingston.

Within this hive we are all alive, With whiskey sweet as honey, If you are dry, stop in and try it, But don't forget the money.

Compared with the cost of a present-day restaurant meal, the old tavern meals were more elaborate, and they cost only a shilling or so.

Light Supper

Roast beef, leg of lamb, cabbage, fat fowl, fresh vegetables in season, ale, port, cherry wine or Barbados rum and brandy.

Breakfast

Veal cutlet, sweetbreads, cheese, eggs, ham, tea or ale or anything stronger to start the day.

The well-known humor of Benjamin Franklin was evidenced whenever he entered a tavern for an overnight stay. Due to general curiosity about all travellers—who they were, where the were from, and where bound—it was the practice of Mr. Franklin to recite something like this: "My name is Benjamin Franklin. I was born in Boston and am a printer by trade. I am travelling to such and such a place. Now! What can you give me for dinner?"

Competition eventually became so great between the owners of the ever increasing number of taverns that the legislative bodies of both New Jersey and Pennsylvania were forced to enact more stringent laws regarding license requirements and the conduct of the establishments. Complaints were general regarding the food and the accommodations in the second-rate taverns.

Few of the old stage taverns still exist. However, one of them, the stone building on the corner of Pennsylvania and Bridge streets in Morrisville, is still intact. The old inn has been restored as it was during days of the stage coach and is now used as a bank.

We met Mr. H. Margerum, who was then the president but is now deceased, and told him about our plans for this book.

He was very excited about our project and spent an hour or so conducting us through the premises.

As we were walking up the staircase we were told it was the original staircase and was refinished as it had been during the early years of the nineteenth century.

On the second floor two small rooms had been converted into a large board room. The board table was of solid walnut four inches thick. It had formerly been the bar top. The Italian marble fireplace, the walls, floor, and chair rails have been restored and now appear just as they did when the tavern was built in 1803. This tavern had been a favorite overnight stop the first night out of Philadelphia.

Mr. Margerum told us that in 1923, when the restoration was undertaken, he insisted that all outside changes must be made without changing materially the original appearance of the building.

4

The First Mile Stones

THE story of the highway mile stones is, we believe, particularly pertinent to the subject of this book. It is believed that one of the first colonial roads marked with them was the New York-Philadelphia road, the King's Highway.

On February 17, 1761, the Board of Directors of the Philadelphia Contributionship Society, the oldest continuously operated insurance company in America, appointed a committee consisting of Thomas Wharton and Jacob Lewis. They were authorized to have thirty-one mile stones made, to be erected on the King's Highway between Philadelphia and Morrisville, Pennsylvania.

On May 15 in the following year, at five o'clock in the morning, the two committee members, the Pennsylvania Surveyor General, and Benjamin Franklin began their journey to measure and place the stones. They started out from the corner of High and Front streets in Philadelphia.

On the right wheel of Franklin's two-wheel chaise was fastened an odometer, one of his many inventions. As each mile was checked off, a mile stone was dropped off to be erected later. Confirmation of the above may be seen in the minutes of the Contributionship Society located at 212 South Fourth Street in Philadelphia. Their museum is very worthwhile. In the rear of the building, in the garden, are displayed several original mile stones, taken from the highways to preserve them.

Franklin's homemade odometer was wired to the top of the axle, on the right side of his chaise. It was set in motion by a hub-type projection on one of the wheel spokes. A photo of that very instrument is shown elsewhere in the following pages, and it is now exhibited at the Franklin Institute in Philadelphia. Franklin sold the odometer to Thomas Jefferson, who was also an inventor and a gadget man. It later became the property of a Mr. William McFarland of Richmond, Virginia, who gave it to the Franklin Institute in 1848.

An interesting footnote to the story of those first thirty-one mile stones that were erected on the road between Philadelphia and Morrisville was that their cost, including manufacture, carving, cartage, and erection, was only thirty-three pounds, seven shillings, and five pence. The stones were five feet high and fourteen inches wide. The mileage and a letter indicating the towns were carved on the face of each stone.

All those original stones between Philadelphia and Morrisville are gone.

Of the stones later erected from Trenton to Elizabethtowne, one remained until a few years ago, when it mysteriously disappeared one night. It was on Main Street in Lawrenceville, New Jersey, and was stone number 36. It stood beside the road on the property of the Lawrenceville Preparatory School.

In the yard of the Contributionship Society there is a stone that may have been one of the original stones on the stage road.

An interesting story about a mile stone and the stage road is about a duel fought at mile stone 4 at Frankford, Pennsylvania. According to tradition, the challenge was issued by Colonel John Laurens, a member of General Washington's staff, to General Charles Lee over the derogatory remarks made by Lee to Washington on the Monmouth battlefield. Colonel Laurens was seconded by General Alexander Hamilton, who was later killed in a duel with Aaron Burr at Weehawken in 1804. Lee was seconded by Major E. Edwards.

The written statements, drawn by the seconds, reflects the polite manners of the day. "On the whole we think it a piece of justice to declare that after they met their conduct was strongly marked with politeness and coolness that ought to characterize a transaction of this nature."

The site of the duel was "in a wooded place situate near mile stone number four on the Point-no Point road."

The only injury from the duel was a slight shoulder wound to General Lee.

When Benjamin Franklin was deputy Postmaster General of the colonies in 1763, in order to provide better mail service on the New England stage roads, he devoted an entire summer to riding in his chaise. He measured the roads with his odometer. At each measured mile a stone was erected.

An interesting history of Old Stratford, Connecticut, published in 1886, written by the Reverend Samuel Orcutt, gives more details of that journey. The Franklin odometer is mentioned, and it is stated that the wheels on Mr. Franklin's two-wheel chaise were thirteen feet in circumference. A mile was registered in each four hundred revolutions.

On the New England journey Mr. Franklin was accompanied by his daughter, who rode throughout the summer journey on horseback.

Our research failed to disclose who made the stones, over one hundred and fifty in number, or who paid for them. Some of the original stones are still intact, but most of them have been stolen or destroyed by widening of the roads or broken by snow plows.

Tavern owners believed that to be located at or near a mile stone was good for business. In their advertising, if the tavern was at or near a mile stone, they so stated. It is said that some of the tavern owners so thoroughly believed the legend that they sometimes dug up one and replaced it in front of their tavern.

The reader may be a bit confused to see, on a mile stone

in Tullytown and two in Bristol, on old Route 13 through Tullytown and Bristol, the letter *T* carved on the top of those stones. They are not the original stones that marked the stage road. They were placed on the road early in the nineteenth century when the King's Highway became a toll road, hence the letter on the top of each stone.

We believe it appropriate to include here a bit of humor that appeared in an interesting booklet, *The Sign of the Hand in Hand,* published in 1928 by the Philadelphia Contributionship Society, copies of which are available at the office of the society on Fourth Street in Philadelphia.

In this fast age, we are little concerned with the old highway mile stones. Our car speedometer tells us today how many miles we have traveled in the past few minutes and, if we are curious as to our destination modern advertising has answered our unspoken question. Huge roadside signs inform us that it is but seven miles to the best chicken and waffle dinner in Joyville, or four and one half miles to Centertown's leading clothing store. To the traveler of a hundred years ago however the roadside mile stones were an unspeakable comfort.

While they cannot properly be called mile stones, there are two other highway markers on the New Jersey part of the King's Highway. One is a sandstone panel in the parapet of the stone bridge over Stony Brook in Lawrence Township northwest of Lawrenceville; the other marker may be seen in the parapet of the old red stone bridge over the Millstone river at Kingston, below the old gristmill.

Both the above bridges were destroyed during the Revolutionary War. The markers were built into the parapets of the bridges when they were rebuilt in 1798.

The Transportation Commission of New Jersey recently announced a plan they feel will help reduce the number of highway accidents in the state. Metal signs will be placed at one-mile intervals on the entire two-thousand-mile-long network of the New Jersey roads.

The idea behind the plan is that such markers will enable state police and others to phone in the exact point of an accident and thus get medical attention and an ambulance faster. Furthermore, the accident records will pinpoint the repetitive accident locations. The King's Highway will be included in the plan and, for the second time in its long history, be marked with mile stones.

While other states have installed similar signs, New Jersey will be the first state to erect such signs on its entire highway system, if the plans are carried out.

We have discussed with highway officials and many other people what actually happened to the old mile stones, other than being broken by snow plows or perhaps stolen for use in private gardens. No one has been able to add anything to the information we already had on the subject.

A few stones may be seen at the Mercer Museum in Doylestown, Pennsylvania, and we found one lying in a farmyard on the Old York Road, which the farmer had brought in to preserve. Others are in use here and there as splash stones under farm pumps.

We were told that in one eighteenth-century house in Pluckemin, New Jersey, much of the cellar floor is paved with old mile stones. We heard of others that are being used as stepping stones in private gardens. We have never seen one for sale in any antique shop, which is strange.

The mile stones served other purposes beyond the marking of the road mileage.

When Benjamin Franklin awarded the first mail contract in 1775 to a stage line, a new method of determining fares and postage was introduced. Both were collected on the distance to the nearest mile stone when the passenger left the stage or the mail delivered, unless the destination was a village in which the mileage was known to the stage driver.

The following bit of whimsical verse is, we believe, a fitting conclusion to the chapter:

Four stones from one rock came,
Differing in goals and aim,
Though their start had been the same.

One became a stepping stone,
Had no glory of its own,
Being just for help alone.

One desired a life of fame,
So a corner stone became,
Bore a burden and a name.

One became a monument,
All to graven praises lent,
Flattering when life was spent.

One became a mile-stone staid,
Showing man where he had strayed,
Back or front looked unafraid.

Thus they chose, and thus they rest,
Which upon this final test,
Served the race of man best.
(McLandburgh Wilson in Frederick Powers,
          Mile Stones and Highways around
                     Philadelphia.)

5

Tales of the Road

WITH the opening of the stage road, many distinguished European visitors journeyed over it to see and write about the emerging new country. They shared the common desire to record, for the folks back home, the story of the strange land called America. Many of their diaries were later published, both in America and in Europe, and they received wide circulation.

From those actual accounts of the road and countryside, we may read today the first impressions of the visitors, recorded as long as three hundred years ago.

The visitors travelled on foot and on horseback, and their principal complaints were about the condition of the road and the few poor overnight accommodations along the way. From their diaries we herein present some of the visitors' impressions and, by so doing, practically, in effect, make the road talk.

William Edmunsen, a preacher, together with a companion, rode over the road many times between Philadelphia and Elizabeth-towne and saw no tame creatures on any day of their journeys. They travelled by day and camped out each night along the road.

When they arrived at the falls at Trenton on one trip, they

could not cross the Delaware River until an Indian boy carried them over in his canoe, with the horses swimming behind on a lead rope. All the written accounts are interesting, but those of Peter Kalm in his diaries, many of which were published in the foreign press, and his later books, are outstanding. Kalm was a professor at the University of Abo in Finland. The primary objective of his American journeys between 1748 and 1751 was to study our flora to determine which type of trees would be adaptable to his native land.

Kalm travelled extensively through the American colonies and in Canada, spending the winters in Philadelphia. He travelled over Indian paths and the King's Highway. He said of our roads that they were good or bad according to the difference of the ground. In sandy soil they were dry and good, but in clay they were bad. He thought the people of America were likewise very careless in keeping the roads in good condition. He pointed out that, if a rivulet is small, they do not bother to bridge it so that travellers could cross it without difficulty. He further pointed out that the small streams, when in flood, actually endangered travellers.

On one trip to Canada, Kalm told of arriving at Bristol, on the way from Philadelphia. He described it as a small village whose inhabitants carry on a small trade and get most of their goods from Philadelphia. Continuing north, Kalm saw many country seats on both sides of the road and great cornfields. He also mentioned travelling through heavy woods for a distance of over four miles and very poor soil on which lupines grew plentifully and succeeded well.

Kalm described the same road on a journey over it in 1745. His comments, in comparison with earlier journeys, are interesting.

Trenton is described as a long narrow town, situated at some distance from the Delaware River on a sandy plain. He pointed out that it belonged to New Jersey and was about thirty miles from Philadelphia. Two churches were mentioned, one for Presbyterians. The houses, he said, were mostly built of stone, but some of them were made of wooden planks. They were commonly two stories high with a cellar below ground with a kitchen close to the cellar. The houses stood at moderate distance from each other and were built so that the street passed along one side.

The gardens, of different dimensions, bound the one side of the houses with a draw well at the end.

Kalm reported that Trenton was very healthy.

His landlord told Kalm that when he first came there, about 1725, there were only a few houses but the town had grown so fast that there were then (1750) over one hundred homes.

In a later reference to Trenton, which for a short time was to become the capital of the United States, Kalm wrote that the people of the town carried on a small trade with goods they got from Philadelphia but that their chief gain consisted of the arrival of numerous travellers between Trenton and New York, for they were commonly brought to Trenton by yacht from Philadelphia or from thence to Philadelphia.

From Trenton the travellers, in wagons that set out every day, went farther overland to New Brunswick.

On the second day of that journey, Kalm further recorded his impressions of the road between Trenton and New Brunswick. He wrote that he never saw any place in America, the towns excepted, so well peopled. Most of the traffic on the road consisted of settlers' wagons and their families seeking new land to farm.

He reported that, as they travelled by horse, they were able to see the countryside better than they would have had they been travelling by covered stage wagon.

Of the village of Elizabeth-towne, he described it as a small town with a rivulet running through it which almost reduced to nothing when the water ebbed away but one which, with a full tide, they can bring up small yachts.

From his diaries one gets the definite impression that Kalm was much impressed with New Jersey. He was particularly impressed with the beautiful Old Brick Church, which he described in considerable detail. The church he saw was, of course, as it appeared before its destruction by the British during the Revolutionary War. It was rebuilt in 1786. Incidentally that church was the first in New Jersey in which services were conducted in English.

Robert Hunter, Jr., a Scotsman, described his experiences and impressions of the road during a fast journey from Elizabeth-towne and Philadelphia in the famous "Flying Machine" in this way; After leaving Elizabeth-towne it was a delightful journey with a view of Staten Island, the Kill, Amboy, and the countryside. Perth Amboy was the capital of the Jerseys and famous for its enchanting situation. Part of the way he travelled through woods and through richly cultivated land. He described the farmhouses along the road, the beautifully cultivated fields and enclosures as vivid reminders of old England. In his opinion, no part of the colonies he had seen resembled England as much as did New Jersey.

Commenting upon the approach to Kingston, Hunter described the road as very hilly and said that it passed through a terrible stony place (the vicinity of present-day Kingston Trap Rock Industries) that was called Featherbed Lane by way of irony.

After crossing the Delaware River at Trenton, Hunter wrote that, after leaving Morrisville, the road passed through a long beautiful avenue of trees followed by the scenic beauty along the Pennsylvania shore of the Delaware River until he reached Bristol, also on the river.

We feel about the scenic beauty of the Delaware valley much as Hunter did on his journey along its shores from Morrisville to Philadelphia. Had he seen the upper valley he would have been very much more impressed but, of course, at the time of his journey over the King's Highway, there were no access roads on either shore of the river in the areas now traversed with many superhighways that permit easy access to that comparatively wild region of the upper Delaware River.

In quite a different vein than the foregoing are these excerpts from the diary of Isaac Weld on a journey he made between New York and Philadelphia near the end of the eighteenth century. He wrote: "There are so few inhabitants, in proportion to the extent of the country, in going from one place to another it is frequently necessary to travel many miles through the dreary woods." Leaving Bristol, he further wrote: "Ten miles further on, opposite Trenton, which stands at the head of sloop navigation, you cross the river. The falls or rapids which prevents boats from ascending any higher, appear in full view as you pass, but their prospect is in no way pleasing. Twelve miles from Trenton is Princeton, a neat town containing about eighty buildings. Here is a large college, held in much repute by the neighboring states. Like all other American colleges I ever saw it better deserves the title of a grammar school than a college. The next town from Princeton is Brunswick containing about two hundred houses. There is nothing very deserving of attention in it. Beyond Newark the country is flat and marshy and there is one marsh that extends upwards of twenty miles. The road is formed of large logs laid close together and, on each side, there are ditches to keep it dry. We met with mosquitos and they annoyed us not a little in passing." Not a flattering picture of the countryside to be sure.

The journals of another visitor, Jasper Danckers, like those of Peter Kalm, have been widely quoted by writers during the past century. Some excerpts from his writing are interesting, even though he was vague about where he happened to be at times. For example, he confused the location of the Raritan River at New Brunswick with that of the Millstone River at Kingston and Rocky Hill.

Danckers mentioned leaving Elizabeth-towne, on his way to Philadelphia, and arriving at Piscataway (properly spelled Piscataway) some four hours later, which was good time on horseback. Despite that, he commented that both he and the horse were not in good shape. His statement to the effect that Piscataway was the last English village in the state was not exactly the case at the time of his journey.

He was impressed with the quality of the farm land along the rivers and creeks he passed.

The approach to Kingston, Danckers described as on a very steep and rocky road. It was necessary to dismount and proceed on foot for many miles until the Millstone River was reached. Some further confusion in his mind was his statement that the Millstone River had to be crossed three times.

On a later journey in 1794, about fourteen years before the first bridge was built over the Delaware River between Trenton and Morrisville, Danckers wrote that considerable quantities of snow had fallen and the keen winds from the northwest had already spread a thick crust of ice over the Delaware River, a majestic stream that is always last to feel the chilly touch of winter. The ice, however, was not strong enough, according to Dancker's diary, to sustain the weight of the stage carriage. Neither was it easily broken, so that when he reached the falls in the river, where it was usual to cross when going from Philadelphia to New York, he had to remain for upwards of two hours, shivering in the icy blasts. However, the diary revealed that a passage soon opened for the boat that was to convey him to the opposite side of the river. Evidently at that time the crossing of the river, even when it was frozen, was generally a matter of considerable inconvenience to travellers. When the frost set in, the slender flakes of ice gradually drifted up in layers over each other. It was only at the most rugged part that a wheeled vehicle could safely pass down the shores of the river onto the thicker ice.

Upon his arrival in New York, Danckers reported that, notwithstanding the the severe cold, he had not been eight and forty hours in the town when every vestige of frost had disappeared and the air was as mild as in September.

As late as the middle of the eighteenth century, from stories told by travellers at the time, it apparently required a lot of faith to convince the average travellers that what they were riding over was in fact a road. One man expressed it this way: "Stumps of trees left for time to consume, yet impede your progress, even on the most frequently used roads between the two largest cities in the colonies. For several miles, immediately before you enter Trenton, the road is so bad the driver,

41

with whom I sat, told me that when his horses became stalled they were sometimes unable to drag the stage wagon over the worst places."

Samuel F. B. Morse, a portrait painter who is better known for his successful invention and demonstration—together with his partner Alfred Vail—of the telegraph, made some interesting observations during a journey from Philadelphia to New York. He wrote that in the journey he and his companions travelled over a very rough road. In crossing a small creek (possibly the Neshaminy), in Neshaminy County. The stagecoach ahead of his left the road too soon and nearly upset in the water. As it was, the water came into the carriage and wet the baggage. According to Morse, it took an hour to get the stage out of the creek. "Next came our turn," reported Morse in his diary. "After traveling a few miles the springs on one side of our stage gave way and let us down, almost upsetting us. We got out with some difficulty and, in a few minutes by putting a rail under one side, we proceeded, jocosely telling the passengers in the third coach it was their turn next."

In addition to the many distinguished travellers, foreign and American, as the previous pages have shown, ordinary settlers and their families seeking land travelled from Manhattan and Long Island; businessmen and traders and dispatch riders were constantly journeying over the King's Highway. During the years leading to the Revolutionary War, members of Congress and dispatch riders used the road. Most of the Presidents of the United States, beginning with George Washington, also travelled over the road during the next two centuries.

With the opening of the first stage lines, early in the eighteenth century, travel expanded rapidly.

The beginning of the French and Indian War in 1754 endangered all the colonies and particularly New Jersey, which placed a heavy tax burden on the inhabitants for the support of England's troops in the long struggle. Being the only vehicular road across New Jersey at the time, the King's

Highway carried the military traffic between Philadelphia and New York.

Of the many illustrious travellers who used the road during the years immediately before and during the eight years of the Revolution, Paul Revere was most frequently seen travelling over it, between Boston and Philadelphia. He carried dispatches on those grueling journeys for the Committee of Safety and made the journeys between Boston and Philadelphia in five days and nights. .

Mr. V. Lansing Collins in his book *Princeton Past and Present,* published by the Princeton University Press in 1931, made some interesting observations about many prominent people who travelled over the King's Highway to and through the university town. He wrote that much of the nation's history and nearly all of the university's (Princeton), from the shadowy days of Taimenend, legendary chieftain of the Delawares, whose lodge was nearby, down to the machine-driven present, could be told in terms of Nassau Street (our stage road). He further pointed out that Nassau Street was a well-worn thoroughfare that made history.

In a further comment, Collins stated that, when the stages stopped at the famous tavern in Princeton known as Jolin's, the coaching traffic reached its height. There were several competing lines making that regular stop, and as many as fifteen Jolly coaches would race off together and a hundred horses would be waiting to take the place of the jaded horses arriving.

Here James Spalding and Washington Irving, immortalizing a visit to Princeton in 1813, set the scene of *The Lay of the Scottish Fiddler,* about an itinerent minstrel who, according to the last line of the poem, long remembered a ghostly visitant of the tavern:

Once a year he deigns to play First a fiddle on Commencement day, When in Jolin's high stately hall Is held the student's annual ball.

43

A fair picture of the increasing volume of traffic that flowed over the stage road, at the end of the eighteenth century and the first half of the nineteenth, is shown in the following account from an issue of the *Somerset County* (New Jersey) *Quarterly* in 1913.

The Van Tilburgh family once owned a large portion of the land on both sides of the stage road in Kingston. They kept a tavern (the Sign of the Mermaid) for several generations.

Before any railroads were built in New Jersey, Kingston was a celebrated stopping place for those travelling between Philadelphia and New York by stage. Forty-nine stages, loaded with passengers, were often seen at the tavern at the same time, and four hundred horses in harness were there to draw upon, one half that number being required to exchange.

Kingston again became the focal point on the road in 1830, when hundreds of newly arrived Irish immigrants were brought there to begin the construction of the Delaware and Raritan Canal, which was begun by the digging of the first lock at Kingston, south of the stage road. The Irish immigrants and their equipment were carried over the stage roads in wagons as there was no other means of transportation to Kingston at that time.

Before and during the War for Independence, members of Congress from New York and Boston travelled over the road to the sessions in Philadelphia. During the war both the British and American armies used the road repeatedly. [George Washington rode his horse over the King's Highway on his way to Cambridge to take command of the American army, and he again travelled the road in 1789, when he journeyed from Mount Vernon to New York to be inaugurated the first President of the United States.

Probably the greatest parade of military might ever to march over the King's Highway was when the French and American armies joined in the march to Yorktown, Virginia, and the victory that ended the war in 1781.

The authors hope the reader will gain a more vivid impression of the road that played so important a part in the development of the American colonies by using the following pages as a guide in visiting the places featured.

6

Interesting Places and Landmarks

ON so many of our highways, particularly those that date back to the time of the early settlements, much of the former quiet and charm has been lost through road relocation and in many instances new superhighways bordering the small communities and even bisecting many of them, to meet the demand of modern traffic. Former small communities have, in many cases, been swallowed up in such improvements or completely wiped out in the building of modern supermarkets and other commercial enterprises.

The above is also true of the King's Highway, the subject of this story, because its route crosses New Jersey, our most densely populated state. For all but a few miles its Pennsylvania portion, along the shores of the Delaware River, is within the city limits of Greater Philadelphia. Despite that, and it is also true in the New Jersey part of the road, there are still many interesting places and landmarks readily available to the motorist who may wish to explore the road.

It doesn't seem possible that so many places are little changed from earlier days, but it is true.

They are listed in geographic order beginning at Society Hill, where the road began. Explore the places and the countryside through which the highway passes, and we suggest additional reading of the material listed.

Society Hill, Philadelphia

Philadelphia and its many interesting historic landmarks are so well known that it seems pointless to cover them herein. However, there is one section of the city that is not so well known. It is Society Hill, now restored to its former condition. During the early part of the eighteenth century the Society of Free Traders bought that part of Philadelphia for development.

During the past twenty years or longer, the entire area became an industrial section and, gradually, over the years, a massive slum. Fortunately, dozens of the original eighteenth-century buildings remained largely intact.

In 1959 the Philadelphia City Council appointed the Redevelopment Authority, originally for the demolition of the buildings of Society Hill. The demolition and restoration of the hundreds of old buildings was one of the most massive and expensive ever attempted by any city. Today many of the former three-story narrow houses have been restored and are again occupied.

The official name of the mile-square restoration is Washington Square East, but the new residents prefer the old name of Society Hill, possibly because of the common belief that the original name was derived from the social status of the early residents.

While Society Hill is a restoration, it is not like Williamsburg, Virginia, and similar restorations around the country. It is delightfully different because it was planned and is geared as a place to live and not as a museum.

Some idea of the massiveness of the Washington Square East redevelopment may be gained from the fact that a square mile of derelict factories, warehouses, and many of the old homes beyond any hope of restoration were demolished. The old Second Street Market and the Head House have been restored by the Philadelphia Council and, now that the restoration of the whole of Society Hill has been completed with its dozens of town houses restored and being lived in, Society Hill is a fascinating place to explore.

The Second Street market was built by the city of Philadelphia in 1745. Head House, as shown at the end of the market, was originally built as a fire house in 1804. The original buildings have been authentically restored by the city and are again a prominent feature of Society Hill.

Old Delancey Street in Society Hill, now completely restored, is an excellent example of the eighteenth-century charm and beauty of the area.

One of the most interesting of the restorations is that of the old tavern known as A Man Full of Trouble. That famous old landmark had become what appeared to be a complete ruin when Mr. and Mrs. William Knauer, prominent Philadelphians, determined to save and restore the building at their expense. It seemed hopeless as the bulldozers were nibbling at its walls; its foundations had sunk into the bed of old Dock Creek, and its floors and dormer windows were practically gone. Today the ancient hostelry appears much as it did two centuries ago. It is now open to the public and is a museum well worth visiting.

The photographs of Society Hill, shown herein, merely hint at the charm of the development. We hope the readers will visit and enjoy this interesting section of old Philadelphia.

The unique and interesting sign that marks the old A Man Full of Trouble in Society Hill. We believe it may be the original sign used when the tavern was first opened in 1759. In any event it is as old as the hand-forged iron work surrounding it.

In the vast restoration of Society Hill this cobbled alley was left as it has been for two centuries or more. The buildings as shown are all a part of the Redevelopment program.

A Man Full of Trouble tavern, now completely restored, on Second Street below the Alcoa Towers in Society Hill. It is now open as a museum.

The odometer owned and used by then Deputy Postmaster General Benjamin Franklin in his survey of the colonial roads in 1753, may be seen at the Franklin Institute in Philadelphia. Courtesy of The Franklin Institute.

Frankford, Pennsylvania

This community, four miles north of Market and Fourth Street near the Delaware River, with its tree-shaded streets and eighteenth-century homes, was on the route of the stage road. It passed through the village on what is today Frankford Avenue. As one drives through it today, little if any of its former charm and quiet is evident.

During the days of the stage lines, several well-known taverns catered to the travellers. Among them was the Jolly Post Boy, of which only a portion of a stone wall in the stable yard remains. There were also the Crossed Keys, the General Pike, and the Rising Sun Taverns, none of which remain today.

Torresdale, Pennsylvania

At Torresdale still stands the Red Lion Inn, which was built in 1730. It has been in continuous operation since it opened and was known throughout the colonies for its gracious hospitality. It is still operated as an inn but today derives its revenue largely from the bar and lunchroom facilities.

It is regretable that this inn that serves the traveling public today—as it has done for 246 years—has been "improved" through the addition in front and the garish sign now displayed.

General Washington and the Continental Army camped overnight on the grounds of the inn while enroute to Yorktown and the surrender of the British on October 19, 1781.

During the years of the Revolutionary War, couriers of many Committees for Safety, on their journeys to report to Congress in Philadelphia, stopped overnight at the inn. Members of Congress from New England and New York also stopped there overnight on their way to Congressional sessions.

On the march to Yorktown, Virginia, and the final battle and surrender of the British in October 1781, the French and American forces canped overnight in the Red Lion meadow while Generals Washington and Rochambeau and their staffs were accommodated inside overnight.

The Fish House

Not far from the Red Lion Inn, on the west shore of the Delaware River and on the grounds of an estate on River road in the Township of Andalusia, stands the Fish House, the little wooden clubhouse of one of the most interesting of the eighteenth-century social clubs of Philadelphia. It was organized in 1732 by a group of twenty-seven fishermen and humorists. Its membership included some of the most notable people of the time. George Washington and Lafayette were but two of many. The club was called "The State in Schuylkill," and it was granted, perhaps with tongue in cheek, extraterritorial rights by the Colonial Governor of Pennsylvania. The members of that unique organization always insisted that their charter actually made them a colony within the larger colony of Pennsylvania.

The first Fish House, a small wooden building, was on the Schuylkill River in what is today a part of Fairmount Park, and it was there that weekly meetings and fish bakes were held. The fish were caught in the nearby Schuylkill and were baked on oak planks, over an open fire.

In 1892 the growth of Philadelphia and other factors made necessary the moving of the clubhouse to a new location on the Delaware River, and later it was again moved farther up the river to its present location, on the grounds of an estate. While the owners of the estate graciously gave us permission to take the photograph of the clubhouse and of the magnificent house that are shown herein, we regret, that for understandable reasons, the estate grounds, the home, and the Fish House are not open to the public.

55

This nineteenth-century house, with its spacious grounds extending to the shore of the Delaware River, was built in 1811 by an exponent of the revival of Greek architecture in America.

The grounds of the estate are not open to the public at any time.

Club meetings are still held regularly we were informed, but the old custom of paying the owner of the land three fish annually in lieu of rent is no longer in effect.

Traditionally the oldest social club in America, the Fish House was originally located on the shore of the Schuykill River and was organized by twenty-seven "humorists" in 1732. It was granted extra-territorial rights within the Commonwealth of Pennsylvania and its members, apparently in jest, insisted that they were a separate colony within the Commonwealth.

It was moved to its present location on the grounds of a private estate on the Delaware River in 1945.

Bristol, Pennsylvania

This small river port settlement was laid out as Buckingham in 1696. The village was frequently referred to by early writers as "a feeble frontier river village without a history." All that changed with the discovery and exploitation of the mineral springs, the baths of which were highly extolled by Benjamin Rush, the Surgeon General of the Continental Army.

When Philadelphia became the capital of the United States, Bristol became still more famous; foreign ambassadors and diplomats made it their summer home. They found the

The Bristol-Frankford Turnpike stone on the old road in front of the Bucks County Rescue Squad building in South Bristol.

This is believed to be the oldest standing Friends Meeting House in Pennsylvania. It was constructed in 1713 in Bristol and in the yard is a sycamore tree that dates back to 1682.

During our visit we were reminded of the words of Charles Lamb's essay in which he wrote: "What a balm and solace it is to seat yourself for a quiet half hour upon some undisputed corner of a bench among the gentle Quakers."

cool river breezes of the village much more comfortable than the conditions in Philadelphia. Many of them built or rented summer homes on Radcliffe Street, along the shore of the Delaware River. As a result, Bristol for many years was one of the most famous watering places in the country.

As one walks along Radcliffe Street today, enjoying occasional views of the river, it is not difficult to envision Bristol as it was two centuries ago, when the illustrious representatives of many foreign nations enjoyed their strolls, in the evening, along the waterfront.

There is so much of historic interest in this old river port that one should plan to enjoy it all, including a visit to the river-front library, built below the level of Radcliffe Street.

The Joseph Head house, north of the Grundy library on Radcliffe Street in Bristol is unique in that it was won in a card game from its original owner by English actor Thomas A. Cooper, Cooper's daughter married Robert Tyler, son of Jonathon Tyler, tenth president of the United States.

The Delaware House

Of the many taverns patronized by the stage passengers, one is still operated near the Bristol-Burlington ferry. It was the first tavern to be granted a license. It was known as the

The original structure now incorporated in the Delaware House at Radcliffe and Mill Streets in Bristol was built in 1705. The first license was granted to the Ferry House, as it was then known, in 1705.

This old landmark is still serving the public as it has for the past 275 years.

Ferry House in 1705 and since that time, following the rebuilding in 1768 when the first tavern was destroyed by fire, it has been operated variously as the George the Third, the Fountain House, and the Delaware House, as it is called today. The inn can be found at 102 Radcliff Street in Bristol.

The historic hostelry well deserves the laurels it has acquired during its long life, not the least of which was the reputation as the finest place to eat between New York and Philadelphia.

John Fitch, the true inventor and builder of the first steamboat, lived in the tavern while carrying on his experiments on the river.

Fitch was not only the inventor, he actually ran scheduled trips with his first steamboat between Bristol and Philadelphia, seventeen years before Fulton's highly publicized *Clermont* was demonstrated on the Hudson River in 1807.

The Stanford K. Runyon house, 910 Radcliffe Street in Bristol was built in 1765. It is the oldest house in Bristol, Pa.

The Friends Meeting House

Another interesting Bristol place to visit is the Friends Meeting House on the corner of Woods and Market streets. It was built in 1704 and, according to the Society of Friends, it is one of the oldest meeting houses in Pennsylvania. William Penn, who spent his summers nearby at Pennsbury Manor, and John Woolman of Mount Holly were frequent worshippers there. The huge sycamore in the yard of the meeting house is, according to the member of the meeting who gave us a tour of the building, nearly three hundred years old. After showing us the meeting house, he suggested that we sit down on a bench on the lawn and enjoy the sunshine and the peace and quiet that always surrounds the Quaker meeting houses.

As we sat there, we were reminded of a quotation from the writings of Charles Lamb that goes:

"What a balm and solace it is, to go and seat yourself for a quiet half hour upon some undisputed corner of a bench among gentle Quakers."

During the eighteenth and part of the nineteenth century, a ferry operated from the foot of Green Street in Bristol to Burlington, New Jersey. Near the landing on the Pennsylvania side of the river, there was a stone ferry house, no part of which remains today.

Legend has it that Aaron Burr, following his duel with Alexander Hamilton, fled from the site by crossing on the ferry, on his way to Philadelphia. We have not been able to find any documentary evidence that the legend is true.

Tullytown, Pennsylvania

The original route of the old road followed the Delaware River on the Pennsylvania side and followed old Route 13 from Bristol and on to Morrisville. The excavations of sand and gravel between Tullytown and nearly to Morrisville have eliminated that part of the original road. It is necessary today to bypass it by using the Delaware River Expressway around that part of the former stage road.

A mile stone with the letter "T" inscribed on it to indicate that the road was a turnpike on the old road south of Tullytown, Pa. The present stones were placed between 1803–1812 during the conversion of the old road into the Frankford-Bristol Turnpike.

The craft shown here is an exact replica of the rowing and sailing barge in which William Penn frequently journeyed to Philadelphia from Pennsbury Manor while in residence there. The boat was manned by a uniformed crew.

Pennsbury Manor

Pennsbury Manor, on the shore of the Delaware River northeast of Tullytown, is wholly a restoration, but it has been rebuilt exactly as it was when William Penn lived there. It is today one of the most impressive colonial estates in America.

The Pennsbury Manor house, and all other buildings that comprise the estate of William Penn on the shore of the Delaware River near Tullytown, are reproductions of the originals that were destroyed by fire.
Pennsbury Manor is now open daily to the public for a moderate fee.

Penn believed that life in the open country was more wholesome than in the city. Accordingly he had plans drawn in 1683, during his first visit to Pennsylvania. When he returned to England, the work on the manor continued under the direction of his caretaker. It was completed when Penn returned for his second visit in 1699, and for two summers Penn enjoyed the country estate, which was dear to him.

After Penn left, the manor house was destroyed by fire. Now completely restored, it is open daily to the public.

In a pamplet given to visitors, who are admitted for a small fee, the manor is described as "This beautiful country house with its spacious manor house and outbuildings, its colorful gardens and neatly kept grounds, and its splendid vistas of the river are imbued with the spirit of the kindly, devout humanitarian who planned it." Pennsbury Manor is a must

The restored carriage block at Pennsbury Manor. They were used by the ladies and children to climb into and dismount from the high-wheeled farm wagons and from carriages before the advent of the automotive age.

for those who seek out places of interest along the old stage road.

Fallsington, Pennsylvania

Nestled in a stand of old trees, miraculously untouched by the burgeoning industries that surround it, Fallsington is today a living lesson in the history of the Delaware Valley.
From a history of Fallsington

On our first visit several years ago, we found it difficult to believe Fallsington was not in fact a wholly restored colonial village. Its stone and frame houses, the store and tavern have been the center of thriving village life since colonial times. The tavern and a few homes are restorations but appear to be originals. As a visitor recently expressed it, "Perhaps the most startling thing about Fallsington is that it exists at all."
William Penn gave the land for the first meeting house in

In their home-made replicas of the dress of the Second Regiment of the Pennsylvania Line, the members of the social club named for the original Revolutionary unit are shown here firing their Brown Bessies muskets in the square at Fallsington.

The Williamson House in Fallsington, Pa has been completely restored and is now open to the public. The original oak-log-siding was covered with clapboards that preserved the original logs. It is now included in the tours of old Fallsington Village on Wednesdays and weekends. The cabin was built in 1685.

The Burges-Lippincott House on Fallsington Square in Fallsington, Pennsylvania. It is one of the seven original buildings in this charming colonial village that are still intact.

1683. The original building was destroyed by fire, and the one now standing was built in 1789 and is now a community center. The other meeting house on the green is still used for worship services. The pre-Revolutionary buildings still standing include the Burgess-Lippincott house, the school house, the old store, and the Williamson house, which was built as a log building, covered with clapboards, in 1650. In a recent restoration, the weather boards were removed, and the oak logs were found in excellent condition. The interior was restored to its original condition. The two huge sycamore trees (bride and groom trees) planted in front of the entrance when the house was built are still standing.

A visit to Fallsington is a memorable occasion on any day but, to really acquire the heightened sense of history a visit to the village will bring, plan to visit it on Fallsington Day, which is observed on the second Saturday in October each year. All sorts of historical pagents and events are a part of

An officer of the "regiment" moulding lead uniform buttons for guests at the "Fallsington Day" observance in the Square.

The first meeting house around which the colonial village of Fallsington was built, was erected in 1690. The later meeting house, shown here, was built in 1789 and is now used as a community house. William Penn worshipped here.

Eager spectators awaiting the firing of the field piece as part of the ceremonies of "Fallsington Day" in the square.

that day. The members of the Fallsington Association and the people of the village and visitors dress in authentic colonial costumes, and everyone has a grand time. The several photographs of one such celebration indicate what fun a visit on Fallsington Day can be.

Today, largely because all major highways, including the old stage road, bypass the village, the small amount of traffic is mostly local.

One may visit the village any day, of course, but the guides who conduct the walking tours of the buildings are available only in the afternoons from March 15 to November 15.

Interesting information about Fallsington may be obtained free by writing to Historic Fallsington, Inc., 2 Meetinghouse Square, Fallsington, Pennsylvania.

Morrisville, Pennsylvania

A post of the Dutch West India Company was established on the Pennsylvania side of the Delaware River, opposite Trenton, in 1624. It is said that one of the fur traders had a unique way to compute the value of the furs the Indians brought in. He weighed the furs on a spring-balance scale suspended from a branch of a tree and, for weights, used his hand (one pound) and his foot (two pounds). The Indians had to be satisfied with that rather unorthodox way of doing business.

Colvin's Ferry was established by an act of the Pennsylvania Assembly on May 13, 1718. It was located just above the present-day Morrisville-Trenton toll bridge. The old stone ferry house is still standing at the ferry site but is in a sad state of disrepair. The owner plans to restore it. During the early years of the ferry operation, the small settlement around it was known as Colvin's Ferry, which later became Morrisville, which it is today.

Robert Morris owned twenty-five hundred acres along the shore of the Delaware River, and his elegant manor house,

Colvin's Ferry House in Morrisville. It was built during the early years of the eighteenth-century. The ferry carried travelers across the Delaware River to Trenton for a century or longer. The building is now a private residence that is being restored.

which stood just below Bridge Street, was the center of his vast business enterprises—including a gristmill, iron forge, brewery, plaster mill, and many others—valued in the eighteenth century at over a quarter million dollars.

The Morrisville bank, formerly a tavern on the corner of Pennsylvania Ave. and Bridge Street, was at one time a popular overnight stop for passengers on the journey over the stage road between Philadelphia and New York.

Morris, using not only his banking connections but also his personal wealth, largely financed the Revolutionary War. For his devotion and sacrifices to the cause of the American colonies, his reward was bankruptcy and a debtor's prison. On February 5, 1798, he wrote to a friend as follows: "My money is gone; my furniture is to be sold; my family will starve and I am going to prison." Such was the reward of that great patriot.

There were two stage inns in Morrisville, one of which was the Robert Morris on Bridge Street near the river, which was still standing earlier in our time but which has long since been replaced by an auto dealer's showroom. The handsome sign, with its portrait of Robert Morris painted by the famous artist

The board room of the Morrisville, Pa. bank has been authentically re-stored and it is today as it appeared when the building was a stage tavern. The long board table is a solid plank of two-inch-thick walnut that was formerly the top of the tavern bar.

Edward Hicks, is now a part of the collection of tavern signs in the Mercer Museum at Doylestown, Pennsylvania. The other inn, a handsome stone building that was the first-night stop for stage passengers from Philadelphia, is still in its original location on the corner of Pennsylvania Avenue and Bridge Street. Some time ago, while we were doing the research and photography for this book, the president of the Morrisville Bank, now deceased, graciously showed us how, in the conversion of the old inn to a bank, the original stairway was left intact, and how two former bedrooms were made into a single larger room creating a board room, leaving all mouldings, baseboard, and other architectural details as they were originally. The fireplace with its hand-carved detail and the Italian marble facing is just as it was when the building was a stage inn. An elegant chandelier hangs over the board room table, which was formerly the bar top of the keeping room of the inn. It is a solid two-inch-thick piece of walnut.

*Summerseat, now an administration building for the Morrisville Public
School system, was built by Thomas Barclay in 1773.*

*Following his disastrous retreat across New Jersey in December 1776,
George Washington was a house guest here for a week or longer, later moving
to another house in Bucks County where he made plans for crossing the
Delaware on Christmas night of 1776.*

Summerseat

Summerseat on Clymer and Legion avenues was built in 1773 as a private residence by Thomas Barclay. Later owners were George Clymer and Robert Morris. Following the disastrous retreat across the Jerseys by the Continental Army in December 1776, General Washington set up headquarters in Summerseat, where he stayed for two weeks. It is believed he began there to plan the historic Delaware crossing on Christmas night in 1776, which resulted in the victories at Trenton and Princeton.

Following extensive alterations, Summerseat is now owned by the Morrisville Board of Education. It is now used as the school administration building.

Trenton, New Jersey

Malcomb Stacy, an English Quaker, was the first white settler in what is now Trenton. He took up a grant of land in 1679 at "ye falles of ye De La Warr" (Delaware River) and built a log cabin and a mill. The little hamlet that developed along the river was first called The Falls.

The only remaining eighteenth-century tavern of Trenton, the Eagle, was built in 1765. Plans are being considered for a complete restoration of the two-century-old building.

WASHINGTON'S RECEPTION BY THE LADIES, ON PASSING THE
BRIDGE AT TRENTON, N.J. APRIL 1789.
ON HIS WAY TO NEW YORK TO BE INAUGURATED FIRST PRESIDENT OF THE UNITED STATES.

Photo made from an original Currier & Ives print showing the welcoming of General Washington to Trenton on his 1789 journey to New York and his inauguration as President.

In 1714 William Trent, an English merchant of Philadelphia, saw the commercial possibilities for water power from the falls and bought 800 acres of land along the river. He laid out a larger town site and called it Trent Town.

The Trent House

This imposing brick house beside the river was built in 1719 by New Jersey Chief Justice William Trent, who occupied it only a short time. It later became the home of Lewis Morris, Governor of New Jersey.

The home of William Trent, for whom Trenton was named, was built in 1719 by the New Jersey Chief Justice, William Trent. The house is perfectly preserved and has been well maintained since the restoration. It is now a museum under the management of the Trent Historic House Commission, appointed by the Mayor of Trenton.

The house is now completely restored and is a museum, open daily for a small fee. Containing largely its original furnishings, it is today a perfect example of the elegant homes of colonial America.

Nearby Assunpink Creek, which flows through the city to the Delaware River, played an important role in the Revolutionary War when, on the night of January 2, 1777, Lord Cornwallis's decision to wait until morning to attack Washington enabled the latter to sweep around the British, leaving their camp fires burning, and surprise another British force at dawn on the Princeton battlefield. The result was a victory for the Continental Army, a decisive turning point in the war. That strategy earned General Washington the soubriquet, The Fox.

A little-remembered fact of Trenton history is that it was, for one session of Congress, the capital of the United States when that body met in a local tavern on November 1, 1784.

Of the many famous taverns of Trenton, only one remains. It is the old Eagle, and it appears today much as it was when it was popular two centuries ago. Plans are under consideration for the restoration of the historic building by the Trenton Historical Society and the Trenton Jaycees.

The Trenton Battle Monument

The Trenton Battle Monument at the intersection of five streets (Warren, Broad, Brunswick, Pennington, and Princeton), is an impressive memorial commemorating the opening of the battle of Trenton at dawn on December 26, 1776.

The Trenton Battle Monument at the intersection of five streets (Warren, Broad, Brunswick, Pennington, and Princeton), marks the spot where the decisive battle was opened at dawn of the Chistmas morning of 1776.

This fine example of Georgian colonial architecture, the Barracks, was built in 1758 to house soldiers during the French and Indian war. British troops, Hession Jaegers, and American soldiers have all been quartered in the building at various times.

While living there the Hessions, after an all night celebration of Christmas in 1776, were routed and defeated in the battle of Trenton by a surprise attack by the Continental Army. The building, now restored by the State of New Jersey, is open to the public daily.

The Old Barracks

Located on South Willow Street is a must for all visitors to Trenton. The imposing sandstone building was built in 1758 to house the troops during the French and Indian War.

It is now a museum, open daily, and it contains a wealth of historic artifacts.

Of the many high points in the history of Trenton, the event that will doubtless always be remembered was the welcome for George Washington on the day he entered Trenton on his way to New York on his presidential inaugural journey from Mount Vernon in 1789. On that journey the General and his party were lavishly entertained, but it is said the reception at the Trenton ceremony surpassed them all. In the photo of the famous Currier and Ives print, drawn on the occasion, which is shown herein, the impressions of that historic occasion are clearly portrayed.

This building on Main Street in Lawrenceville, now a private residence, was once a popular tavern. The tavern ledgers record that Lord Cornwallis stayed overnight here while in pursuit of the Continental Army across New Jersey in 1776.

Lawrenceville, New Jersey

The first settlers of Lawrenceville came to the area from Newtown, Long Island, in 1664. They came by boat through the Sound and the Kills and up the Raritan River to what is now New Bruswick. From there they walked, carrying their possesions on their backs or on horses or oxen if they had any. They followed the narrow Indian path that later became the subject of this story to their new settlement they called Maidenhead, now Lawrenceville. The name was changed to Lawrenceville in honor of Captain James Lawrence in 1816.

Original stage road mile stone that, until recently, stood on Main Street in Lawrenceville, N.J. It has since mysteriously disappeared. It was believed to have been one of the original 1764 stones on the highway.

The Lawrenceville Presbyterian Church was erected in 1764, replacing an earlier building. It is one of the oldest standing churches of that denomination in New Jersey. Lawrenceville was originally known as Maidenhead.

The Presbyterian Church

The beautiful Presbyterian church that was organized in 1698 still stands on Main Street. Within the present building, which was built in 1764, is a part of the original church. The present building is considered one of the most beautiful of the colonial churches in New Jersey.

The Cock and Bull Tavern

Across from the church is a private home, formerly a tavern, which served the stage-coach passengers for a century or longer. The old record books, still in the hands of the owner, record that, while it was a tavern, during the Revolutionary War, Lord Cornwallis stayed there during his pursuit of the Continental Army across New Jersey in 1776. It appears from the records that the petulant Lord liked neither the accomodations nor the food.

The tavern records further show that the parish meetings of the church were held in the tavern, following which all adjourned to the bar. It is understandable as none of the early churches were heated.

Worth's Mill

On the south shore of Stony Brook in Lawrence Township, one of the stone walls of the old gristmill is still intact. The mill, built in 1715, ground grain for the farmers for a radius of forty miles well into the twentieth century.

The famous Keith or Partition Line crossed the stage road a mile south of the mill. The line marked the division between East and West Jersey.

The stage road through Princeton Township and Lawrenceville is lined with beech trees, many of which are over one hundred years old.

This wall beside route 206 as it spans Stony Brook in Lawrence Township is all that remains of Worth's grist mill built by Thomas Potts in 1714. The mill continued operating until the early years of the twentieth-century.

This imposing entrance leads to the campus of the Lawrenceville School with its shaded areas of lawns and interesting architecture.

Lawrenceville School

Lawrenceville, New Jersey

The Lawrenceville Preparatory School dominates the east side of Main Street in the village. The school was founded in 1810, and for generations young men have been prepared there for admission to Princeton and other universities. The tree-shaded campus with its attractive architecture creates a pleasant oasis amid the bustle of the business activity of Main Street.

Across the street is the Jigger Shop, which for generations has been the favorite haunt of the school students. The rather odd name was derived from an ice-cream concoction of the twenties called a jigger. It consisted of ice cream, nuts, meringue, and whipped cream, an approximation of the present-day sundae.

During the days of the straw boater and white flannel

pants, the Jigger Shop was the favorite meeting place of the students. It became nationally known through the stories about the prep school and the students by Owen Johnson and from movie exploits of the students in the film, *Happy Days.*

This graceful three-arch-stone-bridge over Stony Brook in Lawrence Township was built to replace the first bridge destroyed during the battle of Princeton. The present structure was built in 1792 as indicated on the parapet.

Stony Brook, New Jersey

Quaker families were the first to settle in this tiny hamlet, as early as 1693, before the stage road was built. The Clarkes, Fitz Randolphs, Worths, and Stocktons were among the most prominent of those first settlers to take up land there. It was Richard Stockton who purchased a large tract of land from William Penn in 1701. That holding included the land on which Morven now stands in Princeton.

The lower part of this handsome dwelling on the stage road in Lawrence-ville was an early tavern. It was built in 1750 and was known as the Burges-Philips Tavern.

The Quaker Meeting House at Stony Brook, Princeton Township, was built in 1726. It was partly destroyed by fire and rebuilt in 1760. The first settlers of Stony Brook are buried in the church yard.

90

The place of interest in Stony Brook is, of course, the meeting house built in 1726, which was partially destroyed by fire and restored in 1760. Services are still held in the little sandstone building.

Quaker Road as it runs along Stony Brook not far from the stone bridge on the stage road where it crosses the brook. It was here at dawn on that cold morning of January 3, 1777 that General Mercer surprised a British detachment and thus began the historic battle of Princeton.

Princeton, New Jersey

To describe all the places of historic interest in Princeton would require an entire book as has been done by several authors. We shall tell of but a few here.

Nassau Hall

Nassau Hall, the centerpiece of the Princeton University campus, was built in 1754 when the college was then known as the College of New Jersey. It played an important role in

Mid-way to the roof, under the thick ivry shown here on a wall of Nassau Hall in Princeton, a cannon ball penetrated during the battle of Princeton.

The Dean's House in Princeton, originally built in 1756 as the President's House, is contemporary with Nassau Hall. It was built in 1756.

the Revolutionary War housing alternatingly British and American troops. During the battle of Princeton a cannonball penetrated the north wall of Nassau Hall and cut off the head of King George III on his portrait hanging on the wall.

The common graves on the battlefield of Princeton that mark the site where men of both sides were buried following the battle of Princeton on January 3, 1777.

Princeton Battlefield

At the western end of Mercer Street is the battlefield, now a state park, where on January 3, 1777, occurred the engagement between the British and American forces that was a turning point in the war. It was there that General Hugh Mercer was mortally wounded and died twelve days later in the Clarke House on the battlefield. The three-hundred-year-old oak, in the center of the battlefield, stands today as a reminder of that conflict.

93

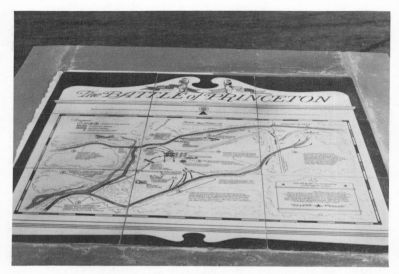

For the guidance of visitors who may want to know how and where the battle of Princeton was fought, the map shown here covers in great detail the placing and maneuvering of the various units during that epic struggle.

The Thomas Clarke house, originally known as the battlefield house, is now a part of the New Jersey Battlefield Park. It was built shortly before the battle and it was to this house that General Hugh Mercer was carried after being mortally wounded. The General died here on January 12, 1777.

The Mercer oak on the Princeton battlefield reputably was standing during the battle on January 3, 1777.

The sculptored facade of the front of the Princeton battle monment on Stockton Street is a vivid portrayal of the emotions of the men who fought that battle.

General Washington seems to be seeing a vision of things to come.

Beside the impressive memorial arch at the edge of the battlefield are the common graves of soldiers of both armies killed in the battle.

Morven

On Nassau Street in Princeton (the old stage road) stands Morven, the home of Richard Stockton, a Signer of the Declaration of Independence. The mansion was built in 1807. It

Morven, built by Richard Stockton, a signer of the Declaration of Independence, is considered to be Princeton's most historic landmark. In 1951 the late Governor Walter E. Edge presented Morven to the state to be the home of the future governors of New Jersey.

stands in beautifully landscaped grounds amid beautiful trees and is the official home of the New Jersey governors.

Senator Clifford Case of New Jersey announced in 1978 that Morven had been added to the list of the National Register of historic places by the National Park Service. Included in the list of other places announced at that date were Barne-

The Henry-Greenland-Joachin Gulick house on the Kingston-Princeton road in Princeton Township as it appears today. Originally the center section with the bow window, as shown here, was a licensed tavern before the beginning of the eighteenth-century.

gat Lighthouse in Ocean County, Absecon Lighthouse in Atlantic County, Old Barracks in Mercer County, and the Old Parsonage in Somerset County.

Morven is believed to be the oldest standing building in Princeton and it is open to the public without charge on Wednesdays.

One of the most remarkable things about Princeton is the fact that, from the battlefield north through Nassau street and the Kingston-Princeton road, there are still standing fourteen buildings the Continental Army passed on the retreat to Jockey Hollow after the battle of Princeton.

For those of our readers who may not be fully conversant with the part historic Princeton has played in the past of America, we suggest further reading of *Princton Past and Present,*. To see and enjoy the many places of interest in this lovely town requires several days or many visits.

The Princeton Cemetery

This cemetery has often been referred to as "the Westminster of America." In it lie the remains of most of the past presidents of Princeton University, a Signer of the Declaration of Independence, Justices of the United States Supreme Court and the Supreme Court of New Jersey, members of the Continental Congress and the Colonial Assembly of New Jersey. In addition, President Grover Cleveland, Vice-President Aaron Burr, and many other notables.

Tusculum, the country home of former Princeton University President John Witherspoon on Cherry Hill Road was built in 1773. The historic house is still a private residence and is not open to the public.

Tusculum

This beautiful stone house, the country home of the Reverend John Witherspoon, a former president of the college, was built in 1773. Witherspoon lived in the house after his retirement from Princeton in 1779.

In addition to the concord coaches used on the Kings Highway after the Revolution, this type of private coach was used by wealthy people of the time. The coach shown here is a replica of the one in which George Washington rode from Mount Vernon, Virginia to New York for his Presidential inauguration in 1789.

Nassau Inn in Palmer Square is not the original building built in 1754, nor is it in its original location. Nevertheless it still has much of the charm of the earlier tavern.

In the Yankee Doodle Tap room are many of the tops of the old round tables on which the students carved their initials. The inn was popularly known as "Old Nass."

101

We remember well the thrilling occasion in the summer of 1939 during Washington's journey from Mount Vernon to New York, where he was sworn in as the first President of the United States, was reenacted. In the reenactment group, which made the journey in a stagecoach that was a replica of the one that made the journey in 1789, were "Washington," "Benjamin Franklin," and others representing the original passengers.

Following their overnight stay in Nassau Tavern, the coach was driven to Tusculum, the former home of John Wither-spoon, where the party was welcomed with a potent drink called Fish House punch. It was served in the same glasses used in 1789.

We were among the guests who partook of the punch in the toast to "General Washington." It was a grand occasion, and we shall always remember it.

Erected by the Daughters of the American Revolution, at the top of the hill in Kingston is one of the several similar markers between the battlefield of Princeton and Morristown on the route of the retirement march after the battle on January 3, 1777,

The Bainbridge House

On the corner of Nassau and Vanderventer still stands the former home of William Bainbridge, commander of our famous ship the *Constitution,* better known as *Old Ironsides.* He was born in this house, and it is today the home of the Princeton Historical Association.

Kingston, New Jersey

Kingston is unique in that it is in three counties and has no central government. North of Main Street is Somerset County and south of Main Street is Middlesex County. At the bottom of Main Street across the Millstone River it is Mercer County.

The stone bridge at Kingston over the Millstone River was built in 1798, replacing an earlier one destroyed during the Revolutionary War. The mill, bridge, and surrounding area, between the river and the Delaware and Raritan Canal, is preserved as a small state park.

103

The Gulick House and the Red Mill

At the bottom of Main Street in Kingston, across the Millstone River on the south side, is the old red gristmill. It no longer operates as a turbine gristmill and is now a private residence. Across the Kingston-Princeton road still stands the Gulick House, which was built at the beginning of the eighteenth century as a tavern. It was there that the Jersey Proprietors met and agreed upon the Division or Partition Line between East and West Jersey. The line extended from the Atlantic Ocean across the state to a point near Flemington in Hunterdon County.

The red mill recently seemed doomed by projected road widening until it was decided to move the new four-lane road down the river a bit and thus save the old stone bridge over which the Continental Army marched in 1777 on its way to Jockey Hollow. As a result, the mill at the end of the bridge was saved as well. Both are now within the small Delaware and Raritan Canal Park, through which runs the stage road.

The original canal lock and toll house within the park are interesting places to explore.

Despite the volume of traffic that passes through Kingston, it still retains much of its eighteenth-century charm.

Washington Headquarters

Rocky Hill, New Jersey

At the top of Main Street in Kingston, by the post office, is a road to the north over which the Continental Army passed following the battle of Princeton. A mile down the road, on the right, is Rockingham, more widely known as Washington Headquarters. It was there that General and Mrs. Washington lived in 1783, while Congress debated the peace treaty in Nassau Hall, Princeton, following the end of the Revolutionary war.

Rockingham, an early-eighteenth-century home, has been restored by the state of New Jersey and, through the efforts

Rockingham shown in its third and present location on route 518 at Rocky Hill. Quarry operations have necessitated the removal of the Washington Headquarters twice.

of the Washington Headquarters Association, many of the early furnishings have been recovered and may now be seen there. In fact, the desk upon which Washington wrote his farewell to his officers, later delivered at Fraunces Tavern, New York City, is one of the most interesting.

The building, due to nearby quarry operations, has been moved three times. Its present site is state land, and the building will not be moved again.

Kingston, New Jersey

Flowing under the King's Highway between Kingston and New Brunswick are a number of "runs," so named by the early Dutch setlers to indicate the distance to tidewater at New Brunswick. They are called the Ten, Six, and Three Mile Runs.

Buccleuch Mansion

New Brunswick, New Jersey

Nearly all of the historic landmarks of the city have disappeared, in the name of progress. However, two such places remain intact. Buccleuch Mansion, a truly colonial mansion, may be reached by driving through the Rutgers campus to Buccleuch Park. Both are along the Delaware and Raritan Canal near Landing Bridge.

The interior walls of the mansion are papered with the original hand-printed French paper.

In anticipation of our bicentennial celebration in 1976 a group of local historians organized the East Jersey Olde Towne Corporation. They planned to raise funds from the interested public to build a colonial village comprised of historic buildings from their original sites throughout New Jersey. It was originally planned to build the village in the very appropriate Buccleuch Park but for reasons we do not know it was built on a two-acre-plot in Highland Park, across the Raritan River. It was dedicated on July 4th 1976 as part of Highland Park's Bicentenial celbration.

Old Queens

New Brunswick, New Jersey

Royal Governor William Franklin granted a charter in 1666 for the establishment of Queens College in New Brunswick. The name of the college, now a state university, was changed to Rutgers in 1825. It was so named in honor of Colonel Henry Rutgers who donated the bell that still hangs in the tower of the original college building. Today the first building of the college is used as an administration building. It is built of New Jersey sandstone that the years have left in perfect condition.

The charter for Queen's College in New Brunswick was granted by Royal Governor William Franklin in 1766. Old Queens, shown here, was the first substantial building of Rutgers College. It is now used as an administration building.

This attractive building in Piscataway village, with its traditional columns and tall steeple, is typical of the early nineteenth-century churches. It was built in 1837 replacing an earlier structure that was destroyed by a tornado.

The original bell that was made in England hung in the belfry of the first church that was on the same site. The bell now hangs in the belfry of the present church.

Some of the head stones in the church yard of the Episcopal church in Piscataway village date back to the late seventeenth-century.

St. James Episcopal Church

In the village of Piscataway in Piscataway Township is a beautiful old church built in 1837. The present building replaced an earlier church destroyed by a tornado. The bell in the tower was made in England in 1724 when it was made for the original church.

In the church burial ground are some headstones that date back to the seventeenth century.

Merchants and Drovers Tavern

On the corner of Westfield and St. George Avenues in Rahway still stands the old tavern that was very popular with the drovers and other stage passengers for many years. It was one of the many stops General Washington made on the way to his inaugural in New York City in 1789. The restored tavern may be visited the first Sunday of each month and at other times by appointment.

Behind the larger and more pretentious Merchants and Drovers Tavern is the Terrill Tavern, now being restored. During the Revolutionary War, the Terrill Tavern was used alternately by both the British and the American military forces. It may be seen only by appointment during the restoration.

Elizabeth, New Jersey

John Ogden and a few friends were the first to settle at the site that would later be the terminus of the King's Highway. They landed in the fall of 1665 and and established a new settlement on Newark Bay, as it is now known.

A few years later Philip Carteret brought thirty more people from England to join the first settlers. He named the tiny settlement Elizabeth in honor of his wife Lady Elizabeth. It later became Elizabeth-towne and is today Elizabeth, an industrial center.

First Presbyterian Church

Broad Street, Elizabeth

Old First, as the church is better known, was formerly topped by a ninety-foot steeple that was destroyed by fire many years ago. The church is still in its original location on South Broad Street, and it was in this church that the first

Old First Church, now one of the most famous of the New Jersey landmarks and the first church in New Jersey where the services were conducted in English, is still standing in its original location in South Broad Street in Elizabeth.

Surrounding Old First Church on South Broad Street in Elizabeth is the old burying ground in which are interred the remains of many famous early Elizabeth settlers. It is also the resting place of over 100 Revolutionary soldiers.

services in English preached in New Jersey were held. In the churchyard are the remains of over one hundred soldiers who died in the Revolutionary War.

Baldwin Locomotive Works

Elizabeth, New Jersey

There is no trace of the little machine shop in which Matthias W. Baldwin built the first successfully operated steam locomotive. It was first demonstrated by Thaddeus Stevens on his estate at Hoboken. It was called the Stevens Steam Carriage and was the first to be operated in America.

Liberty Hall

Morris Avenue, Elizabeth, New Jersey

This prestigious landmark is being included in this tour even though the buildings and grounds are not open to the public.

Liberty Hall is one of the most impressive of the early American estates left in New Jersey. It was built in 1773 by William Livingston, the first governor of the consolidated Jersey provinces. It is privately owned and is still occupied by a private family. Alexander Hamilton lived in Liberty Hall, as a guest of the Livingstons, while a student in Manhattan.

General and Mrs. Washington were entertained overnight in Liberty Hall on the way to his inauguration in New York. Mrs. Washington made an extended visit, and her trunk stands today at the foot of the bed in which she slept during that visit.

Liberty Hall is furnished like a museum, largely with the possesions of several generations of the family now living on the estate.

During its early years the hall was a very popular place and was the scene of many gay affairs. The list of notables who were entertained there reads like an early Who's Who.

112

Among them were John Jay, the first Chief Justice of the United States. He was a frequent visitor and in fact married Livingston's daughter Sarah. William Henry Harrison, President of the United States, eloped from Liberty Hall with the Governor's stepdaughter, Anna Symmes, in 1795. Generals Washington and Lafayette were frequent dinner guests while the Continental Army was nearby, during the War for Independence.

The extensive grounds of the estate, like so many places of historic value, have been overrun by the public. They have left their litter and, in fact, have damaged many of the ancient trees on the grounds. As a result, a tight security is maintained over the building and the grounds, night and day, to keep the public out.

Boudinot Mansion (Boxwood Hall)

1073 East Jersey Street, Elizabeth, New Jersey

The Boudinot Mansion was built in 1750 by Elias Boudinot, the first President of the Continental Congress. The mansion played a tragic part following the battle of Springfield on June 23, 1780 when the British, who had killed the Reverend James Caldwell, pastor of the Springfield church, tossed the body of Caldwell on the front steps of Boudinot Mansion. Such brutal acts were a warning to the colonists to give up the struggle.

Later in 1781 James Morgan, the British sentry who shot Parson Caldwell was tried in the Westfield church and was convicted. There is a fifty-cent admission.

Boxwood Hall or the Boudinot Mansion, as it was also known, was the home of Elias Boudinot, the first President of the Continental Congress. Following the murder of Parson Caldwell by the British the body was tossed on the porch of the mansion as a warning to the American Patriots.

Belcher-Ogden Mansion

1046 East Jersey Street, Elizabeth, New Jersey

This restored building was built in 1750 by the Royal Governor Jonathan Belcher. The house has been authentically restored and is open to the public by appointment.

Nathaniel Bonnell House

1045 East Jersey Street, Elizabeth, New Jersey

Built by an original "Associator," (early settler) this house is reputed to be the first house built in Elizabeth-towne. N. Bonnell, a French Huguenot, was one of the early settlers.

The Bonnell House may be seen any day without an appointment. It has been completely restored and is used as the state headquarters of the Sons of the American Revolution.

114

The home of the Royal Governor of the Province, Jonathon Belcher, who lived in it from 1751 to 1757. The Governor was one of the first supporters of a school there that was the begining of the College of New Jersey. This school later became Princeton University.

The Bonnell House, built about 1670, is believed to be the first or second oldest house in Elizabeth. It was recently restored and is now the State Headquarters of the Sons of the American Revolution.

Conclusion

Near the beginning of the nineteenth-century the King's Highway was extended to and through Newark, Hackensack, and over the Hackensack meadows to Bergen Point on the Hudson River. Through the marshy areas tree trunks had to be laid over the road to avoid the sinking of the vehicles in the soft roadbed.

The place on Newark Bay at Elizabeth-towne Point where the first settlers of that area landed in 1665. It later became the eastern land terminus of the stage road from which travelers continued to Manhattan by ferry.

Thus, the entire route of the road finally became passable for the stages and other vehicles. The short ferry ride across the Hudson River from Bergen Point saved much time on the Philadelphia-New York journey, compared to the route to Elizabeth-towne Point and the long journey on the sailing ferry to the Battery in New York.

In 1848, when the railroads began operating on routes that paralleled practically all of the King's Highway, the stage lines gradually lost business until there were so few passengers most of the stage lines ceased to exist.

Thus ended the excitement and drama engendered by the thundering stages and gallant drivers.

In conclusion we would like to repeat a sad lament that the unemployed stage drivers often expressed. It was used in one of our earlier books, "Along The Old York Road," that was published in 1965. The former drivers expressed their feelings about the railroads in the following manner:

Oh, it's once I made money by driving a team Now all is hauled on the railroad by steam May the devil catch the man that invented the plan For it's ruined us poor wagoners, and every other man Now all you jolly wagoners, who have got good wives, Go home to your farms and spend your lives. When your corn is all cribbed and the grain is sowed, You will have nothing to do but curse the railroads.

Suggested Reading

Bailey, Rosalie Fellows. *Pre-Revolutionary Dutch Houses and Families in Northern New Jersey and Southern New York.* New York, N.Y.: Dover Publications, 1968.

Battle, J. H., ed. *History of Bucks County, Pennsylvania.* Philadelphia, Pa.: A. Warner & Company, 1887.

Benedict, William H. *New Brunswick in History.* Privately printed in 1925.

Bill, Alfred Hoyt. *A House Called Morven.* Princeton, N.J.: Princeton University Press, 1954.

Bowers, Claude G. *The Young Jefferson, 1743–1789.* Boston, Mass.: Houghton Mifflin Co., 1945.

Clayton, W. Woodford. *"History of Union and Middlesex Counties, New Jersey.* Philadelphia, Pa.: Everts & Peck Publishing Co., 1882.

Collins, Varnum Lansing. *Princeton, Past and Present.* Princeton, N.J.: Princeton University Press, 1954.

Dunaway, Wayland F. *History of Pennsylvania.* New York, N.Y.: Prentice-Hall, Inc., 1948.

Earle, Alice Morse. *Stage Coach and Tavern Days.* London, England: Macmillan Co., 1900.

Faris, John. *Old Trails and Roads in Penn's Land.* Philadelphia, Pa.: J. B. Lippincott Co., 1927.

Field, Edward. *The Colonial Tavern.* Privately printed in 1897.

Forbes, Esther. *Paul Revere and the World He Lived In.* Boston, Mass.: Houghton Mifflin Co., 1942.

118

Garber, John Palmer. *The Valley of the Delaware.* Port Washington, N.Y.: Ira Priedman, Inc., 1951.

Green, Doron. *A History of Bristol Borough in the County of Bucks.* Privately printed in Camden, N.J., in 1911.

————. *A History of the Old Houses on Radcliffe Street, Bristol, Pa.* Privately printed in 1938.

Hart, Virginia. *The Story of American Roads.* New York, N.Y.: William Sloane Associates, 1950.

Hutchins, Rev. S. P. *Bristol Pike.* Philadelphia, Pa.: George Jacobs Co., 1893.

Kalm, Peter. *Travels into North America.* 3 vols. Translated by John Rienhold Forster. London, England, 1772.

Kull, Irving, ed. *New Jersey: A History.* New York, N.Y.: American Historical Society, Inc., 1930.

Lane, Wheaton. *From Indian Trail to Iron Horse.* Princeton, N.J.: Princeton University Press, 1939.

Langer, William L., ed. *An Encyclopedia of World History.* Boston, Mass.: Houghton Mifflin Co., 1948.

Lathrop, Elise. *Early American Inns and Taverns.* New York, N.Y.: Robert McBride & Co, 1926.

Lee, Francis Bazley. *New Jersey as a Colony and State.* Publishing Society of New Jersey, 1902.

Leiby, Adrian C. *The Early Dutch and Swedish Settlers of New Jersey.* New Jersey Historical Series. New York, N.Y.: D. Van Nostrand Co., 1964.

Lippincott, Horace Mather. Early Philadelphia: *Its People, Life and Progress.* Philadelphia, Pa.: J. B. Lippincott Co., 1917.

Melish, John, comp. *Traveller's Directory through the United States.* Published by the Philadelphia Society, 1802.

Niemcewiez, Julian W., *Under Their Vine and Fig Tree.* Newark, N.J.: New Jersey Historical Society, 1916.

Onswake, John. *The Conestoga Six-horse Bell-Teams of Eastern Pennsylvania.* Cincinnati, Ohio: Effert 2 Richardson, 1930.

Orcutt, Rev. Samuel. *A History of Old Stratford, Conn.* Stratford, Conn.: Stratford Historical Society, 1886.

Philadelphia Historical Society Bulletins, 1916–1966.

Piscataway Township [N.J.] *Anniversary booklet, 1666–1966.*

Powers, Frederick Perry. *Mile Stones and Highways around Philadelphia.* City History Society of Philadelphia, 1922.

Public Roads of the Past. Washington, D. C.: The American Association of State Highways, 1953.

Rich, Wesley E. *History of the United States Post Office to the Year 1829.* Cambridge, Mass.: Gordon Press, 1924.

Scharf, Wescott. *History of Philadelphia.* Philadelphia, Pa., L. H. Everts Co., 1884.

Shumway, George; Durall, Edward; and Frey, Howard. *Conestoga Wagon, 1750–1850.* Williamsburg, Va.: Early American Industries Association, Inc., 1964.

Snell, James P., comp. *History of Hunterdon and Somerset Counties, New Jersey.* Philadelphia, Pa.: Everts & Peck Co., 1881.

Studley, Miriam V.. *Historic New Jersey Through Visitors' Eyes.* New Jersey Historical Series. New York, N.Y.: D. Van Nostrand Co., 1964.

Thayer, Theodore. *As We Were: The Story of Old Elizabethtown.* Elizabeth, N.J.: New Jersey Historical Society and Grassmann Publishing Co., 1964.

Tyler, Donald H.. *Old Lawrenceville.* Privately printed at Lawrenceville, N.J., in 1965.

Van Horn, J. H., comp. *Historic Somerset.* Somerset, N.J.: Historical Societies, of Somerset, N.J., 1965.

Wall, John Patrick. *New Brunswick over a Century Ago.* Newark, N.J.: New Jersey Historical Society, 1911.

Westager, C. A. *Dutch Explorers, Traders and Settlers in the Delaware Valley.* Philadelphia, Pa.: University of Pennsylvania Press, 1962.

Young, John Russell. *Memorial History of the City of Philadelphia.* 2 vols. New York, N.Y.: New York History Co., 1895.